Critical Acclaim for *Second Nature*

"*Wait? What? A* Second *Nature?*"
—*Ralph Waldo Emerson*

"*So this one time? At band camp? I tried* Second Nature?"
—*Michelle Flaherty*

"Second Nature *is the source of all true knowledge.*"
—*Leonardo da Vinci*

"*Pain is temporary,* Second Nature *is forever.*"
—*Leonardo DiCaprio*

"Second Nature *brings a smile to my lips.*"
—*Mona Lisa*

"Second Nature. *Hot.*"
—*Jean-Luc Picard*

"*Oh, man!* Second Nature! *Why didn't I think of that?*"
—*Gary Snyder*

"Second Nature *is as familiar to me as the path around Walden Pond.*"
—*Henry David Thoreau*

"*I'm tidally locked in a face-to-face embrace with* Second Nature."
—*The Moon*

"*I don't always blurb poetry, but when I do, I prefer blurbing* Second Nature."
—*The Most Interesting Man in the World*

Also by Eric Paul Shaffer

Poetry

Kindling: Poems from Two Poets, with James Taylor III   (Longhand Press, 1988)

RattleSnake Rider   (Longhand Press, 1990)

Portable Planet   (Leaping Dog Press, 2000)

Living at the Monastery, Working in the Kitchen   (Leaping Dog Press, 2001)

Lāhaina Noon: Nā Mele O Maui   (Leaping Dog Press, 2005)

Road Sign Suite: Across America and Again   (Obscure Publications, 2007)

Restoring ~~Lady~~ Liberty   (Obscure Publications, 2009)

A Million-Dollar Bill   (Grayson Books, 2016; Coyote Arts, 2024)

Even Further West   (Unsolicited Press, 2018)

Green Leaves: Selected & New Poems   (Coyote Arts, 2023)

Free Speech: poem sequences   (Coyote Arts, 2024)

Fiction

You Are Here   (Obscure Publications, 2004)

The Felony Stick   (Leaping Dog Press, 2006)

Burn & Learn, or Memoirs of the Cenozoic Era   (Leaping Dog Press, 2009)

Criticism

How I Read Gertrude Stein by Lew Welch, edited and with an introduction
    by Eric Paul Shaffer   (Grey Fox Press, 1996)

Second Nature

poems

Eric Paul Shaffer

"a practice natural enough to look natural"

Coyote Arts

Second Nature: Poems. Copyright © 2026 Eric Paul Shaffer

Cover and book design by Jordan Jones

Cover image: "China's traditional Chinese painting ink in the mountains," by May - stock.adobe.com. Used by permission.

Author photograph © 2025 Michael Blanchard. Used by permission.

Photographs on page 10: "The Terror of War" by Nick Ut, public domain; "Kim Phuc and Thomas, 1995" by Anne Bayin.

"A June Afternoon with Michael" appeared as a dedicatory poem in Michael Adams. *Dancing at the Crossroads: Last Poems: 2010–2013* (Grand Junction: Turkey Buzzard, 2022).

All rights reserved. No part of this publication may be reproduced, stored in a retrieval system, or transmitted in any form or by any means, electronic, mechanical, photocopying, recording or otherwise without the prior permission of the publisher.

Library of Congress Control Number: 2025951323

ISBN   Paper   978-1-58775-060-1

        E-Book   978-1-58775-061-8

1 3 5 7 9 10 8 6 4 2

Coyote Arts LLC
PO Box 6690
Albuquerque, New Mexico 87197-6690
coyote-arts.com

for my brother

J.B. & me

Dark Matters

Field Trips	3
Perseid Meteor Shower, Oʻahu	5
The Ones Who Didn't Know	6
Once, A Mango Tree	7
The Creaking of the Net	8
That Girl on Fire	11
Traci's Sunset	12
On Giving You the Shirt Off My Back	13
Travel Notes on Bells in Japan	14
A Few Words for Jesus	16
One for Sorrow	17
A June Afternoon with Michael	18
Flappy	19
A Gift from a Collector	21
On My Love, Losing Her Hearing	22
Don't Mention It	23
September 10, 2001	24
A Tree Newly Planted in the Islands at the End of the World	26
Dark Matters	27
A Blessing for Companions Who May Never Again Share a Table	28

Extremities

My Red Watch Cap	33
Small Town Affairs	34
The Economy of Signs	35
My Balderdashery	36
Steering Into the Skid	38
Traffic Accident on Main Street	39
Top Ten Bumper Stickers for American Poets	40
Poet Lesson #53: How to Pick Up a Lover	41
On Contemplating a Celebrated Cover of *APR*	42
Exfinition	43
Eight Points at the Navajo Bunkhouse	45

Extremities 46

God as a Dispenser of Pez 48

The Murder Weapon 49

My Plea of Not Guilty 51

Yet Another Dream of Gary Snyder 52

A Lasting Mark, Dark and Greasy, on the Ballcap of American Literature 54

The Purple Earth 56

A Yearning for Misspelling 57

When I Can No Longer Stand What Is Broken 58

Home Truths

Instead of Writing Poems Today 63

King Tide 65

The Poor Box 66

Self-Portrait at Birth 67

The Life and Death of Somebody's Son 68

And This Is for You 69

My Old Football Injury 71

Angry at the Wind 73

Wedding Photo: September 8, 1954 75

The Eleventh Street Irregulars 76

Surrounded by Sky 78

The Glazier 79

Parsley 80

Joe Dickie's Last Hallowe'en 81

Scabs and Other Childhood Lies 82

Orphaned at Sixty 84

Cigarettes in Paradise 85

Hiking the Fire Access Road 87

What My Brother Might Say as a River 88

You Little Bastards 89

And Now, After *Second Nature* 91

Notes 94

Acknowledgments 99

Dark Matters

travels through days and darkness

Field Trips

I was not only a little in love with Miss Nichols, so when one day she told us
Robert Kennedy and his wife Ethel were her friends, I wanted to believe her,
but I wasn't sure. I was nobody, and she taught sixth grade in a cinderblock

school beyond the borders of the district, so how could *she* be anybody?
Yet Kennedy was a name in history and news, and from my window, I could see
the dome of the Capitol and the pale needle of the Washington Monument.

I knew we lived close to power, but I thought the voltage flowed through webs
above our heads on poles in black wires stitching the suburbs to the light.
The rowdy class challenged her, so we marched broad halls to the phone

in the principal's office. She spun the dial and handed me the black receiver.
"This is my friend Ethel Kennedy," said Miss Nichols, and I said hello. "Hello,
what's your name?" I told her. She asked, "What are you studying in school?"

And I answered her as I answered my parents, "Nothing." There was silence.
She wasn't as pleased as my parents. There was no more to say, so I returned
the phone to my teacher. She patted my hand and smiled.

Later, she arranged
for us to meet Robert Kennedy in the Attorney General's office. He was loud,
a small, jovial man in a large room, but what I remember most was the ruddiness

of his complexion and a loose thread on his sleeve. Our homework was to scour
the newspaper for a serious question to ask the man Miss Nichols called "Bobby,"
so as a token of my love for her, I gathered my courage and raised my voice,

"What do you think of President Johnson's war on poverty?" And he saw me
for that one moment. He spoke encouraging words I wish I remembered now.
At the door, he shook each of our hands. My hand. Maybe it was Miss Nichols,

too, who took us on a field trip to the U.S. Mint, where we watched green ink
and linen become the currency of our nation. The man at the mint held $10,000
over our heads, and let us each hold the bill for a moment. The paper was stiff

and new, ridged with green, the fingerprint of wealth in one open palm. I wonder
now at all of the silliness we believe of the past. Hope and questions of why not
or why are for the future, and we forget that fate is an illusion born of looking

back. No fate elected I would witness flames rising between America's needle,
thimble, and me, but I did. In those elementary days, I was not fated to become
as inarticulate as my dull response to Ethel Kennedy on the phone. Bobby was

not fated to be shot by a misguided man whose fame I refuse to speak. Nor was I
fated to grow as rich as briefly holding a ten-thousand-dollar bill in the sixties
seemed to promise, and never were we fated to hold whatever now fills our hands.

Perseid Meteor Shower, O'ahu

for Naomi and Michael

For the last three nights, I've urged friends into darkness
        to see stars fall. Not one of us has seen a streak,
    a spark, or a flicker. The moon swells as the days pass,

and the stars themselves dim in the reflection from that steady,
serious, gray and white face. And then, from the coast, the clouds
        trail the wind, crowding the stars into thin cobalt canyons

and coming between us and the quick vision of rock and flame
we seek, lying back in the grass with only us between the planet
        and everything else. I expect a lot from the sky, I guess,

and I want to give the universe every chance to come through
for us, yet I awaken to rain and a sky blank with clouds glowing
with the light we cast against the night. Not all that falls burns

or brings light, nor is all above clear to us, waking or dreaming.
        We rise to walk through rain and sky, abandoning stars
we cannot see to the night and the long, lovely business of fire.

The Ones Who Didn't Know

One or two on trampolines were among the first not to know
the ground had begun to shake. The ones speeding over highways

knew, for concrete was suddenly as slick as winter ice. Yet the ones
idling at intersections waiting for the light felt nothing
as rubber tires and steel springs stilled the shaking. Not all the ones

who were asleep woke to a nightmare. Whether the beds were soft
or sleep was deep, a few sailed on in bliss. Drunken ones

stumbled dully along with other ones walking or running
as the unbound land rocked beneath all their varied gaits. Dancers
were unaware for a few last steps, and the music swallowed

the screams of the first to know, before the power failed and glass
shattered. The ones in love knew immediately,

and called for their lovers, but many, lost within noisy, private
passions, knew nothing of others for whom the earth
had begun to move. Falling, the single suicide heard the wind

as laughter, one more element forsaking him, even as the earth
drawing him swiftly down rippled like the face of the sea.

Once, A Mango Tree

I miss the mango tree cut from the neighbor's yard,
                gone now for a thousand days. On a shelf
above my work, I keep a single leaf retrieved that day

from the lane between us. The leaf is brown and stiff,
        the only evidence of a mango tree once green and tall,
yet I can still taste the ripe ones I found lying by the fence.

        Let me go out on a limb here, and say nothing good
ever came from chainsaws, and cutting down trees
        never made the world a better place to live.

        The street is hotter. The dogs have no shade. Water
bowls are dry in the sun. And someone's cutting down
        another tree today. The men sing as they work.

Once in a while, I hold the leaf before my eyes close
        enough to eclipse the place where my neighbor lives.

Behind that single leaf in my hand, the mango tree lives on.

        While the crew slash at the tree, dropping limb
after limb, I wish the tree a dying triumph, yet one more life

is gone again. Some of the dead are trees, but I accept all
        the losses. The older I get, the more there is to lose,
                so every day, I practice opening my hands.

The Creaking of the Net

                        The sun is rising, and the stars are already gone,
or there is too much light from our star to see those fainter points
            at this hour, early, with the fierce white rays slanting
through jalousies and the air chilly enough that I actually feel

            the weight and warmth of fusion from ninety-three
million miles away. The sky doesn't need the sun though blue
arises from the rays. The sea doesn't need the shore when tides
grind new land to sand. The Earth doesn't need us while nothing

remains of us without that blessed dirt. How embarrassing to recall
now that truth at night, when I exit the tunnel on the Pali Highway
            headed toward Kailua town and glimpse that black expanse
of unlit ocean between the stars and the rows of hundreds

            of golden points, like knots on a net, that are each
a streetlight on one of the straight rows of my home, I remember
            again that humans huddle, tangling family and friends
and work in grand webs of avenues and motives and highways

and ends that seem to strangle the lives anyone can live there.
I understand the fury of Jeffers and Snyder with us as we ignore
            the crowding and the thrashing and the creaking of the net
drawn in. We have looked so long and often to the shadows

            at the edge of vision for friends or foes or lovers or all
                        that we are unable to see, that nothing is there
but more light. Even with the day surrounding us now, I see little
            as I face our silly, fragile failure to survive when survival

is so easy, even with the impediment of intelligence blocking
the way. The light will not leave us alone, even when the day
             ends. We have lived too long with contempt
for the sun, ignoring the radiance until the light burns us.

"The Terror of War," Vietnam, 1972

"Kim Phuc and Thomas, 1995," Canada

That Girl on Fire

for Michael Blanchard

On Christmas Day, after we dined at Denny's,
I saw a photograph of a woman in a magazine.
She was that girl on fire, who, glazed with napalm
and nothing else, had run flaming and screaming

from a Viet Nam village in one of those wars.
I remember when I first saw that grainy moment,
hating the photographer for snapping the shot
rather than running to help. Now, in a new black

and white revelation, over the artful draping
of her garment, her left shoulder rose, rippled
with scars, and on her arm was her sleeping
child. That round infant face was full of peace.

The moon, also ravaged by fire, was somewhere
in the sky. Too many think the moon is always
full and only visible in darkness, but tonight,
the old moon holds the new moon in her arms.

Traci's Sunset

for Traci Winegarner, 1959–2016

That evening, we sat in the cellphone lot. The low rumble
of the pickup idling beside us throbbed through the glass.
       Aunties in the cab laughed and cooed over a baby
whose crying pierced reggae and rock from radios clashing
in the dusk. In our silence, I named this one Traci's sunset
while day faded over black mountains.

             When the sun rose
this morning, she was petting cats, sipping coffee, making
a shopping list for the barbecue, and watching an upcountry
      morning awaken. Now, that same sun was sinking
into the waves, and the last day she had ever seen was done.

Airliners and egrets emerged from the glow on the runways
and disappeared over the darkening island and darker sea.
      On the orange horizon, silver clouds were turning
pink, pink flushing to rose, rose to purple, purple thickening
to black, and the blue over all deepening until the first stars
      shone their long, thin light into our eyes.

           The racket
of traffic beyond the fence was blurred, and the chain link
      diamonds between us and the last of day sheared the sky
into a puzzle. At that moment, far behind us, shadows trailed
the rays of the sun climbing the slope of Haleakalā, gleaming
      once at the peak as the Earth turned away from the light.

On Giving You the Shirt Off My Back

for Alice Marie Hamilton

Not only that you asked for this shirt I bought in Bali, but I knew
you'd treasure an immaculate garment — sleeves, buttons, pocket,
and collar — more than I will. Having worn it in and out of trouble,

through tight spots, beyond sunshine and shade, and in hard places,
I pass this on to you. Though I adore the sharks in gray and black,
mouths agape and grim, bellies glimmering in the fabric of pacific

cobalt and coral waves, I knew you saw deeper. Of all the shirts
on that noisy street, this one, worn well, was a glib bit of fiction

between me and a holiday world, a batik of sleek images I donned
to distract the vendors, tourists, locals, guides, and inevitable lost,
from a man buttoned within the open-throated ocean. But the shirt

you saw concealed easy mystery, in blue profound enough to be
black, emerging in a shape so simple that even a man like me
paused on a noisy market sidewalk to lift the shirt from the rack,

check stitching and seams, and start to barter. In your first glance,
you saw in the lines and figures the meaning of the man dyeing

the fabric, the woman who cut the cloth, the children who sewed
the buttons and released the exact and hangered form. Now, I send
you, at last, this shirt, creases precise and collar pressed, no worse

for the wear since that day those sea shades of white, black, silver,
and hues of blue caught my gaze, and I halted my morning walk,
raised the material to the sun, and purchased instead of passing by.

Travel Notes on Bells in Japan

Apparently, in a rain-streaked journal of my travels
in Japan, I wrote: "At the monastery is a surprise, and a bell
                 is the source. Beneath a typically pitched red roof

is a great bell beside a hammer-beam hung from the rafters.
To ring the bell, a monk draws back the rope-wrapped pile
                          and lets the wood fall on the metal curve."

Reading these words, I recall days lost in a din of years,
             that even ringing a bell is done differently in Japan.
                          In the West, we hang

             a tongue in the open mouth, and rock the bell
till the clapper wags. In the East, the metal curve is struck
with a wooden shaft, a play of elements that frees a voice.

And I've forgotten these words: "The tones of a beaten bell
are cleaner, deeper, cross the hills, resonate among pines,
             buzz between green needles, linger in the beds

of streams. The rocked bell sounds from inner turmoil,
tongue working, wagging as the world shifts, a cry rising
             and falling as the mouth turns and returns."

             Are these notes mine? Copied from a book?
How did I forget my own scribbling while I recall morning
             sun and dust motes gliding through the busy temple,

the clapping hands of old ones, the clatter of coins,
             the hiss of buses at the stop, scents of incense
and pine, the long concrete skyline, and the dark sea beyond?

Again: "We simply make too much of the different ways
                        we do the same things. A bell is still
the open mouth of music awaiting the touch of the world.

Rocked with a rope or banged with a beam, a bell sounds
            and resounds with the strength of the vessel
        and the strength we bring to bear on the material."

At the bottom of the page, near a sketch of bell and beam,
I wrote, "There is a tale of a clever man who, when told
        to sound the bell, replied, 'A bell is too deep for that.'"

A Few Words for Jesus

Lilies toil not and neither do they spin because lilies
are flowers, and even what we think of as beauty is not
        a purpose. The colors are neither designed

nor intended to delight us into wasting whole days
reclining in a grassy field of contemplation, or worse,

snapping the stems so we can display the petals
in a vase to decorate supper. And, no, we need no more
        swords. We have enough and enough spears

and crowns and crosses. We need more fish and loaves.
Nor need the poor always be with us, for if we force

the rich through the eye of a needle, we have enough
to share, and we will always have enough. And no,
        we cannot abandon the ones we love to walk

along the seashore with you because our nets are cast
for fish. And yes, I know you don't want to be touched,

        but we must. We must touch each other. For you
and we need to learn well and to remember skin is not
where each of us ends but where the world embraces us

one breeze, one beam, one splash at a time. Fine, come
        as quickly as you wish, but you need not rush.

We are morning mist vanishing from blades and leaves,
        and wind barely ripples the fields as we pass.

One for Sorrow

after the nursery rhyme

The gold-billed magpies of the Sacramento Valley
were fat, strutting every field and green as I ran late
to classes, but returning to campus twenty years
              later, I saw only one. Some plague
cleared the valley, and the magpies are mostly gone.

A single magpie is rare and we, knowing the birds
mate for life, assume the worst, and so, sorrow.

Now, with only one to watch, the lore of magpies
is all I recall. Someone told me once magpies bode
ill fortune, but like us, bring the bad news home.

            And one, some say, attended the birth
of some savior, an advent speaking yet of sorrow.

These plump, pied rascals once swaggered through
parks and yards, black and white with rainbowed
wings, and a friend once mistook one for a cat
stalking a sparrow through the grass. As the poet
           never said, but now is true: the bird is flown.

The college quad is a desert but for students lying
on a well-mown lawn. I want to teach these children
doom. I will say a magpie recognizes a reflection
           in a mirror but does not gaze as long as we.

But I am silent in dull spring sun among my myths.
One is enough for sorrow, yet none enough for more.

A June Afternoon with Michael

remembering Michael Adams, 1949–2013

After three thousand miles, I arrived in late afternoon, and we met
again, two men and a dog in a room lined with books both had read.

Through that easy afternoon, we spoke of lines, men and women,
and cities and mountains we had known and loved, and in the way
of unwound, unremarkable hours, we slowed, drowsed, and napped,

nodding in our chairs, our conversation slipping to the floor and fading
like the day, and something woke me, something in that warm room

of quiet breath and wood and pages, something like a train whistle,
and then, I felt, as much as heard, the long, slow, comfortable rumble

of great weight rocking tranquilly down the line, and in that moment,
as evening arrived, my thoughts were of good American steel, straight
and sound, set well on creosote and crossties by hard, skilled hands,

and I saw untold miles of tracks to the sun lingering red in the west,
the last light gleaming on those shining silver rails that take us home.

Flappy

for Debi Wylie, 1953–2016

After the accident, Veronica opened the darkened
      house. The clatter from the cage was quick.
"Bite me," said Flappy, useless wing beating
      the bars, the black bead of one eye
reflecting the last of the day, "Grab a beer."

Descending from telephone and power lines,
      Debi had found the injured myna
in weeds beside the blacktop. Installing cable
upcountry meant ascending poles on old roads
through wide, silent fields of zucchini, papaya,
      lavender, horses, and goats penned
in the shade of kiawe.

      As a gift, she gave herself
the bird, coming home to mend the broken wing,
offer food and water, in a house where I dropped
      by for a beer. "What's his name?" I asked,
peering into the cage. She pulled her cap down,
      raised her eyes, and grinned. "Flappy."

"That's a *terrible* name," I said, and she replied,
      "Yeah." That Saturday, when Ashley killed
Debi and Traci at Makani Road with her speeding
silver car and mad desperation, we found laundry
wet in the washer, the cans and boxes for dinner
      on the kitchen counter, six hungry cats,
and, of course, one mad, scrappy myna.

Wet clothes went in the dryer. We returned food
                    to cupboards and cleared the table
              for the chores demanded in the sudden task
of forever closing a household. "Oh, shit, oh, damn,"
              croaked Flappy as we packed and discarded.
Even crippled, what we love may outlive us. "I love
              you," he squawked, "Kiss my ass."

A Gift from a Collector

I played with the change in my pocket as my old teacher
spoke. The vaulted room was hot, the bulbs were lofty,
and the dim light was lost while the evening descended.
The chairs were rigid under comfortless cushions, angled
for agony, and I pinched a finger between bent, square
steel frames when I shifted in my seat. Afterward, I met
my teacher once more, and I was glad to see and speak
to him after so many years, so many miles, so many small
spaces lived in and through, all the brief boxes of rush
and expediency. Then, as we laughed, he tilted his head
back and regarded me. "Do you remember Rose?" I didn't.
He reminded me of a bewildered student thirty years back.
I'd tried to help by giving Rose some well-intentioned
bad advice. I'd forgotten. He remembered. My finger
throbbed. I thought again of boxes I've packed, kneeling
in a small box of rooms, and then unpacked in a new one,
of all the boxes stuffed with reams, bills, and coins. Boxes
can't contain what we forget to pack, so I don't remember
forgetting that moment, that lost girl, that witless mistake.
But here now was my little, long-ago lapse, mine again, old
but still shiny, worn smooth by years, and returned to me
in my change, like a collectible coin stamped with a date
and a "D," now to be cast in a clear plastic cube, for display
near a nameplate on a broad oak desk or in a mahogany
bookcase among certificates and degrees, conveyed to me
by one who carried that trim-rimmed minute long and far,
hoping for a moment he could press that penny in my palm.

On My Love, Losing Her Hearing

Music rings a booming room, but you don't hear the song.
      Waves bending the air no longer ring your ears.

At the concert, the air throbs with chords, from musicians
      who cannot play for us, yet the hall blooms

with flames from raised lighters. Bone in your jaw, eroded
by years, fails every breeze, every word you wish to hear.

      Sound is a burbling spring of surprise, now capped.
You hear only what you see, so I try to see what you hear,

cupping my fingers over my ears. The hollow world roars.
      At night, in bed, I still say, "Did you hear that?"

      And you smile when I remember too late. "No.
What did you hear?" I tell you, "A Barn Owl flying over

      the Kawainui." A dawn you no longer hear my voice
may come, but I will always speak, always to you, always

      tell you everything. I will speak when our eyes meet.
And I promise to sit through the silence in the din around us

            and hold your hand.

Don't Mention It

The scat on the trail is here to stay. We step over, not around,
the pile. The vultures overhead are the same or different ones
who scored the blue yesterday. After all, who but a vulture
can tell one vulture from another? That's just the way it is.

We kick up the dust. The cloud settles to earth unless wind
catches it, then it settles somewhere else, but it always settles.
Look at the mountain. If you can see it, it's here. If you can't,
it's still here. What you see means nothing to the mountain.

And that's why I'm here, boots, bottle, and bandana. This rock
recalls those who made the place sacred. I have no intention
of dying as poetically as they did. Those poems are written,
and I'm not going back. I will leave rooms crowded with books,

shoes, and other belongings someone else will have to discard.
No sweet, solitary death for me. I come to this place to ponder
this little mystery. I'm glad we're here today. We stopped a fool
from killing a rattlesnake on the trail. We told him we'd go to jail

before we watch one more creature killed when we could save it.
The trail becomes a place when we stop walking, and rattlesnakes,
lichen, manzanita, and vultures are bound to be here. We insisted
he thank us for our surly wisdom and for not kicking his sorry ass

down the mountain. He left angry; we kept climbing. Vultures
glide above, as significant as everything that circles. Death is grim
for those who die, but for the rest of us, a day like that, or like this,
is just another day, and today, the sky is just as blue and beautiful

or blank as the people around us can make it. A lookout tower
of stone and timber tops the peak. The door's locked. We're here.

Eric Paul Shaffer

September 10, 2001

in Kula on Maui

That upcountry evening, I carried
    a battered wooden milk crate
from the garage up the two-track weedy lane
    to the hilltop beyond the house
to watch the sun set. The fields were still,
    and as I passed, so were the leaves
of jacaranda, brilliant purple blossoms long
    gone. The kiawe tree had gathered
    all of the night to come
beneath low, shadowed branches.

    Zucchini lay swollen
and green on the mounds from south
    to west. The sky over Haleakalā
    was cloudless. The sun hovered
over waves in the Kealaikahiki channel
    between Lānaʻi and Kahoʻolawe,
and the air shone with alpenglow, a luscious
    pink from horizon to horizon lasting
for hours, or seeming so. The light did not fade.

    The rosy gleam simply trilled
from sweet to delicious, and my skin
    grew luminous in what passed for time
as the stars entered, one by one. Beside me,
    the mountain glistened a shade
of watermelon subtly deepening, redder
    and richer while dusk endured.

I lingered at the crest of the hill
until the path disappeared, and I could see only
the sky. The next day, the world ended.

A Tree Newly Planted in the Islands
at the End of the World

My salt will not nourish the future, but grief, like rain, seeks
       the earth, so I'll plant this tree and water the roots, weeping.
Black crescents of dirt will rise beneath my nails, revealing

       again how the work of our own hands graces us with soil.
This tree will grow well beyond my life. These leaves will gather
light born in the heart of our sun ten thousand years ago, vaulting

from that radiant surface to this in eight minutes. I will never know
       ten millennia inside an orb of only light, but I can understand
a few minutes of crossing darkness before joining an explicable

chemical mix of green and wind, root and limb. Water nourishes
       what we plant in the rays from above. Yet light does not fall.
Light rises. From a core, burning for billions of years toward an edge

       we'll never see, even with all this light. The ground glows
around my shadow as I bury new roots meaning more than this day
ever will. Light needs no meaning, but I do, so I will follow water,

       into the earth, compose and decompose as time ensues, even
as the planet rotates and revolves and whirligigs through the galaxy.
Even as the islands flourish and fail around us, I can add no more.

Dark Matters

As I pull late into the garage, I extinguish the headlights.
Darkness leaps toward me, warm, silent, intimate. For one
            inglorious moment, I regret there is no hell.
So many deserve a sulfurous sojourn. I fumble for a handle,

step from the car and the garage, and the stars burn, fierce
and mute overhead. Orion is poised with his shield and club
confronting the bull. In six million years or not, the stars
            sketching his figure in the night will explode, spilling

atoms and elements into the universe that will one day
compose another life that will never know any one of us.
More of the ones I love are gone, but the hunter hefting
            his weapons is here, for a few more millennia at least.

            I'm glad I will not be here to mourn their passage,
and the stars will surely not mourn me. Staring up, I ponder
the believers in an exclusive gated heaven, a rainbow bridge,
blue lights, a white light at the end of a tunnel, a planet

of one's own, seventy-two white raisins, or a golden field
            beyond an azure sky, but all of that means less now
than the breath to tell the lies or the ink to write the words.
Dark is the night. The street beneath the constellations

            is unlit, and leaves rattle down the street in the grip
of the wind. In the house is a single light, and I know
my love waits within for me. I wish on the dark beyond
the stars for yet another dawn to share with her before the day

            I stop and return the sun-forged elements of my body
to the future that, long after I'm gone, they will illuminate.

A Blessing for Companions
Who May Never Again Share a Table

Let us bless this bread with our fellowship and the clatter of silver,
the tinkle of glass, and the laden thunk of plates upon the board. Let us

speak of the events of the day: the tanager among the pines and prayer
flags, the daisies growing beneath the cold, blue surface of the lake,

the full moon that means more to us tonight than ever before. Let us
break the bread with our hands and pass the loaf through the circle

for each one of us to share what completes our meal. Let us raise our eyes
to each other and lift our glasses without a toast but with glad and silent

recognition that our gathering on this evening is brief and bright, a swift,
slow passage, the quick flit of a falling star through summer constellations

that will outlast the light and the fire. Let us remain here in conversation
and quiet and the fading light until we must, at last, sleep, and let us not

know fully what our departures from this table mean until we are each
on a way we truly mean to take. And when we look back, as since we are

human, in our strength and our frailty, we must look back, let us happily
recall that as we parted, our final words to each other were "Fare well."

Extremities

deviations from rectitude, etiquette, and orientation

My Red Watch Cap

on a walk with Bill

In Portland, a huge Goth guy, leather, chains,
gleaming with spikes and buckles, locked eyes
with me, and when I nodded, he rasped, "I like

your hat." Everyone does. A beaming hue,
the shock of nothing less than hibiscus struck
by lightning, my red watch cap draws attention

like a scarlet spark in the eye of Heaven. I stride
along las vegas ways, glitter when I walk,
and wave to citizens of my millennium, my era,

my nation, and I am elevated like spirits rising
from a single shot of George T. Stagg at the Red
Star Tavern. My head glows with rare regard

from street, sidewalk, people, and panting dogs.
Topped by my coruscating cap, I am a match
without peer, keen, poised, and ready to strike.

Small Town Affairs

When he started dating his brother's wife, everything went to hell.
I guess dating isn't really the right word. He was having an affair
with her, and they weren't careful enough to conceal their love.

They rubbed against each other at family barbecues and kissed
each other goodbye a little too long after church. They met

"accidentally" at the mall for long lingering lunches at IHOP.
When the romance was finally revealed, everybody in town was

"surprised." Ladies whispered in beauty salons. Pickups idled
in the middle of Ash Street, driver's door to driver's door,
as gossip crossed the center line, spreading like a lemonade stain

on a picnic tablecloth. Everybody knew both men, from boy
to man, and they knew the two well. He and his brother were
brothers. They did everything together. They hunted moose

and mink. Together, they fished and flew radio-controlled
model airplanes. One had a Hellcat, and the other a biplane,

but nobody could remember which had what. They bought
the same car, well, not the *same* car, but the same model,
racing each other on Main Street like a drunken fraternity

of two. Dad was proud they were men's men, but they were
Mama's boys and never argued about who Mother loved best
while each forking down three slices of her Dutch apple pie

every Fourth of July. After the inevitable, the sheriff asked
why he would do such a thing to a brother he'd loved all his life.
He said, and I quote, "Love means nothing when you're in love."

The Economy of Signs

one for Jordan Jones

In buzzing orange neon,
the sign in the store window said,
      "GAS LOGS."

The possibilities were obviously endless.

      "Gas logs?" I said.

We regarded each other with the frank amazement
      of the economically uninformed.

    Reflective, he said,
"You know somebody actually called
a sign company and said,
      'Yeah, we want a neon sign
         for our store window.
      Can you make that in orange?'

      'Uh-huh,' the sign guy said,
      'What's it supposed to say?'

      'Gas logs.'

And you just know the sign guy said,
      'Say *what*?'"

My Balderdashery

Yeah, if a haberdashery is where Leo goes mad mixing mercury
        and leather to make hats, I'm building me a balderdashery.
That's right, my friend. I'm constructing a shop where I will

just make shit up, where I make my own way as I stumble, stagger,
strut, and sprint along headlong with a pen, paper, and a belt looped,
        draped, and decked with tools to measure, cut, frame,

and finish whatever the hell I make of language. The cornerstone
shall be a boulder of blarney. How much bolder? Just enough.
Some carrier of hod, hooey, and horse puckey will bull bricks

across the yard, slather mortar for a wall or around a magnificent
empty hole where the sheer wonder of a window will someday
        be glazed, lifted, caulked, and gazed through. Do you see

what I mean? The walls of my world will be sure. The foundations
will be square. All the lines will be plumb, blue and true, forthright
and straight-forward, for when I pluck the chalk line, the unvarying,

unbending score on the floor will be plain, and the rest will be right
as plane, saw, hammer, nails, knuckles, and backs bent to the task
can make a place. And there, I will whip and wind, ravel and sew

millennial and majestic apparel suitable for a page of any dimension,
east or west. Quality material will I cut from whole cloth, sewing
my pieces together with stitches that curve and weave seams sturdy

and steadfast. Get thee to a bookery. I'm busy. Do you not see
        I'm atoil in my balderdashery? I only have work to do,
and I have work to do. Here's the fine mess I make of the swaddling,

suits, and shrouds I fabricate. Go! I imagine that among volumes,
quartos, broadsheets, and fascicles, someone will find something to fit
your flab or flatness to a habit, stiff, bordered, and black and white

      print on a page in any book that covers you. Yes, they'll say,
that sentence makes you look taller, and that paragraph takes years
from your face. Clearly, you are yet wrinkle-free and unblemished

beneath beams of sun or moon. See? The only crease in your visage
is the valley between recto and verso, and no, that chapter definitely
      does not make your ass look big. Go, be garbed in the work

I've already ribboned, ruffed, and buttoned. At least, for the sake
      of all I tuck, taper, and trim, step back. Get out of my light.

Steering Into the Skid

Once upon a time, steering into the skid seemed like right
action on black ice or a frozen bridge, but in the middle,
the car does what a car will do, and I am a hapless voyager

at the mercy of forces without. Sitting in the driver's seat
and gripping the steering wheel makes no difference
       in a car on ice. Sliding in a direction I did not know

       I was going, I watch trees spiral by the windshield,
guardrail approaching, other traffic slewing and slamming
brakes to floorboards to erase what is clearly my mistake.

I wish for guidance, for patience, for fortitude while speed
peels away, friction barely present where tongues of rubber
and ice meet in a flat bare landscape slipping sideways

like the power we think we control because we tendered
the cash. And that tree, vertical and final, is not moving;
the car is moving, with power I pressed into the engine,

power missing the kiss of traction, power I dreamed
I controlled, could control, when now the only everything
       in my hands is a wheel I cannot turn swiftly, slowly,

or delicately enough to stop what I started. A world of bare,
black limbs, gray sky and concrete, and white whirls beyond
this vehicle beyond my control, and I was once the driver.

Traffic Accident on Main Street

The street is nowhere to meet someone you've known
all your life, and of all, that broad concrete is nowhere

       to find your uncle sprawled, bloodied and dazed
by whatever event leaves us to lie on our backs at noon
across the centerline. Hit by a bus or a bike, the man

       is prone, with the entire world behind his back,
and, for a moment, I'm able to imagine the planet directly

above him as he lies at the lowest point on the globe
       hanging from the drooping curve like a tear
about to fall. The gathering weight of the world grips

and suspends him above a cloudless blue thin and bright
enough to conceal the 13.7 billion light years between him

and the edge of the observable universe. One good turn
deserves another, but when his breath fades, I can see
that he nor we nor I will get another. Maybe passing away

expeditiously is best, even dying among idling engines,
congested traffic, and a distant, impatient tooting of horns.

I can't think of anything he or we or I have done badly
or well enough to require a return or irrevocable dismissal
to paradise or inferno. The street is scattered with accident

debris and familiar blank faces over bent necks, crowding
around to look down on him with the same mean thought.

Top Ten Bumper Stickers for American Poets

one for the Fire Gigglers

How's My Writing? Call 1-800-EAT-FONT!

I—Break—For—Emily—!

Praise The Word!

Keep America Beautiful! Please Put Literature In Its Place!

I'd Rather Be Rhyming!

If You're So Smart, Why Ain't You Anthologized?

I ♥ New Works!

My Other Book Won A Pulitzer!

Honk If You Love Whitman!

If You Can Read This, I'm Published!

Poet Lesson #53: How to Pick Up a Lover

First, get a car.
>It should be reasonably clean, inside
>>and out. Dentless. Cool, if possible.
Fairly new or fashionably old.

Next, cruise.
Drive streets a new lover might walk:
near the library, the post office, the mall, the university,
>>the bank, the grocery store.

Finally, roll slowly to a stop. Don't honk.
>>Wait for a glance. Smile.
>Say, "May I give you a lift?"

Most important:
Leave a dog-eared copy of Dickinson's *Complete Poems*
>>on the passenger seat.

On Contemplating a Celebrated Cover of APR

"Many bad poets are incredibly ugly.
Some good ones are, too."
—*Mark Strand*

In black and white, the evidence is irrefutable:
poets are ugly people. Perhaps ugly is too harsh.
Their hearts are hidden hells, but the ravaged,
twisted, melted faces—yes, freakish is more apt.

Is a repulsive visage the requisite, unfortunate
complement to a poetic soul, or is the vessel
of the golden voice misshapen by the molten
radiance within? Let's hope it's not the worst.

Let's hope it's not that poets are not born but made
by schoolyard bullies, disappointed parents,
		reluctant lovers, and an inexhaustible cast
who batter, crush, and shame children into the slim

comfort of a world of words, where salvation
is a blast of clever lines in a cloud of bad breath,
solitude, darkness, close companions who are
only animals, and the telling absence of a mirror.

Exfinition

after a painting by Ernest Williamson III

Always outside of ourselves, the world looks just so
when we travel far enough. Inked and painted lines
        are ours, drawn from us, not the sky,
not the earth, not even the whorls at the tip of a finger.

Look softly, and the world blurs. Edges vanish. I slacken
        my sight and exfine the world, erase brinks,
mute borders, and *then* I see. In a fade of red, I see a world
in flux. In a mist of green, I see what I should never expect.

        In a splash of white, I see an eternity
no one wants. I see all the same way snow smooths
the verge of a cliff and deroughs the peaks of mountains.
        The way fog dims wet windows and dulls

every particular of trees and telephone poles, banks
and cathedrals. The way clouds, mere miles above the sea,
        obscure billions of years of light or the quick
flicker of meteors enticed to ground, yet let fall the rain,

each drop englobed by the same force in a foolish rush
        to earth. The way a sky so delicate
and blue overhead suddenly blackens as we thrust ourselves
to icy heights beyond the blunt thinitude of what sustains

        our breath. The way the wind slides rocks
over slick, wet desert sand in curving trails, explicable
and unstuck. The way red becomes a younger red
        we call pink and in another light is gray.

The way future planets infusing rocky shards and elements
resolutely decline the perfect circles we first sketched
                in heliocentric shells. The way impermanent
stars drift from the monsters and heroes traced with sticks

on ancient darkness. The way the land in aerial photographs
                melds in a winding of rivers and arching
of mountains. The way the boundless gyres in the energetic
rainbow shimmer of oil on water. The way sleep submerges

                whatever I think I am in what I think I am
not, and I see no more of myself before I rise once more
from those blank waters. The way bubble gum and grass
                harden in a sidewalk wad, then soften

in summer sun. The way medieval artists severed peasants
and knights, hovels and haystacks, pigs, goats, and horses
        at the canvas edge to reveal the world goes on.

Eight Points at the Navajo Bunkhouse

"Did you hear that?" The buck stands,
        head raised, ears erect. *"Listen."*
And he turns to the earth for nourishment.

"Be bold," says the robin.
              Bounce, bounce, stand.
      "Be so common no one sees you."

The mountain says, "I am light radiant
          with light. Watch this."

"I'm taller than the mountain," says the pine
            to the walking man.
      "I'll show you. Come closer."

The creek says, "My rush is the patience
       of ages. At my heart is the way
          the salmon walks home."

"Raise your limbs to the sky," says the fir.
      "Be compassionate. Start here."

In an open pack, the spider weaves a web.
      "I'm at home wherever I work."

      "Keep your feet on the ground,"
says the spruce. "From roots in darkness
      rises everything that loves the light."

Extremities

Yesterday, my mouth ran off, talking serious trash about me.
I frowned on that crap, but what could I do? My eyes were
quite blue, and they wandered down the street. Glancing

back, they could not bear the sight of me, welling with tears
and tearing around the corner. Will I ever see them again?
My nose thinks I stink. My ears won't listen. I'm falling apart.

My nipples always suspected they were useless accessories
beneath the fuzz on my chest. They finally decided my T-shirts
rub them the wrong way and flipped out. They think I'll miss

them, but I don't care. Those are two little pink circles I can live
without. My belly, much to my surprise, remains, a round mound
of flattery, still depending on me. What a waist. But my hair,

well, my hair was the first to go. Then, my penis slithered down
the sidewalk, looking to hang out with someone more interesting
than I am. My belly button just gaped. My hands got a grip

on each other and let the fingers do the walking, disappearing
arm in arm. My toes tapped nervously twice and inched away
to become part of someone they can believe in, except, of course,

the big toe on my left foot, which I know is only supporting me
to make a point. My chin is sticking it out, too, leading me
into a world populated by sullen former appendages now sulking

in Jerry Springer's green room to make celebrities of themselves,
confronting me on national TV with my failures to keep myself
together. All my far-flung bits labor to forget the surly pile

of pieces, which is all that is left of me now that my best parts
have gone the way of all flesh. Under the circumstances,
I thought my legs would stand by me, but they were essentially

divided, went their separate ways, and now, I don't have a leg
to stand on. I've taken up Zen, and I'm sitting a lot, which,
hopefully, hides my embarrassment now that I'm half-assed.

God as a Dispenser of Pez

He is on display with Thor and Goofy and Bart and Santa, all hung
                 from steel posts in bags of crackling cellophane. I behold
His pale angry face over the paler flowing beard, a faded flame
aimed at Earth under a thunderous gaze. I recognize Him across
a dark press of centuries, from glowing illustrations in illuminated

tomes and the ragged plaster on Renaissance chapel ceilings. I see
lightning blue eyes, deadly and determined, fixed on whatever
hapless human strays through His downward gaze. The white
brows are thick, set in the scowl we expect. His nose is a scimitar,
                 the classic blade hung by a thread above our heedless heads.

Yes, I've seen the image He forbids: One enthroned in azure and black,
in stars and clouds, shadows casting the slanted beams of "God light"
                 sought for religious cards and calendars. His fierce face caps
the teetering pillar of universal blue embossed with three divinely
                 capital letters. I ponder the hidden spring within, pressing

the candy tight beneath the clamp of His jaw and chin, flat at the root
                 of the tongue, like His first words calling forth light. I consider
the pastel stack of sugary bars emerging into the world as they drop
into the maw of time or mine. I unwrap a pack, scented of strawberries
and honey, slip the pieces into place, forcing each down, then lower

                 the immutable, celestial head. Without arms, atop a skinny,
cerulean column, He is less formidable. With only a thin plastic
pediment, He looks tippy, easy to topple, ready for a fall of His own.
I take Him easily in hand, snap back His head, and with my teeth,
                 brick by sweet brick, I tear the candy from His throat.

The Murder Weapon

In innocent hands, this is a Louisville Slugger, wood
with gently curving grain, spun to a balanced cylinder
seeking a lazy game, a ball, and a perfect pitch. Here is
a screwdriver from his first complete set, ready for work
but only too close to hand at the wrong moment. A lamp,

a hammer, a hoe, a vase, a crowbar: all have a purpose
that isn't the last for which they were employed. A car,
a chair, a bottle, a rake, a set of shears: nobody means
to use these tools for impulsive, lethal tasks, but they do.
These are the weapons of desperation and inspiration.

Then, there are the weapons that leave us wondering
if the choices reveal too little imagination or too much:
a flagstone, a bit of cinderblock, a plastic bag, a stapler,
a shower curtain, a nail gun. These are the weapons
of an irony that spills like blood after the fact: the son

kills the father with the Boy Scout knife he received
for Christmas; the wife stabs the husband with the slice
on which she served their wedding cake; the mother
sinks the minivan in the lake, drowning her daughter
in the car seat she embroidered with the girl's name.

Some weapons are simply an opportunity of landscape
and circumstance. The edge of the cliff on the scenic
overlook for a view of migrating whales, the car idling
in the sealed garage, the radio blaring reggae on the edge
of the bathtub: all present a sudden, overwhelming answer

that immediately asks the question. Witnesses are witless
or absent or drunk or stupid or all of the above. Testimony
from any one or more of a foolish gaggle reduces the jury
to laughter or to scorn. On the same ledge or on the same
bathroom tile, jurors know accidents do actually happen.

And then, there are the hands themselves, those beautiful,
delicate, fluttering birds of purpose and flair, intention
and achievement, left alone, empty or full of nothing
but rage that reaches out and closes around a tender neck
or folds into stones knobbed with knuckles thrown

and thrown again and again against the face, the flesh,
the curves of the body, and the desires we crave. Even
our hands are weapons, traitors to our dearest, earnest
urge to touch another, our hands, once only offered, shy
and eloquent with the gentle hope to hold another hand.

My Plea of Not Guilty

I am the ambassador of my past, and my constituents are the dead
men and boys who once were me. On the floor of our parliament,
standing on rich burgundy carpet, within these marble halls
and mahogany walls, the blue glass-paned lamps cast this day
$\qquad\qquad\qquad\qquad$ within the chamber,

I embody their interests, good intentions, bad ideas, youthful whims,
ignorant follies, the drives and desires of body and mind in each
green minute passed before this hour. I ask all of you, from the near
counties, cultivated, comfortable, and lush, and the far countries,
lands of winding rivers and grand, gray ranges, to hear my plea.

$\qquad\qquad\qquad$ Forgive me for what I am, for what I am is
a tally of tattered ballots cast by a three-year-old, an eleven-year-old,
a twenty-seven-year-old, and all my sunny younger selves, every one
of whom I could now convince to campaign, canvass, poll, survey,
and vote otherwise for the sake of our common future. I am bent

beneath the bulk of countless choices made by boyish versions of me
who did not know what they did, and did not know what I know now,
$\qquad\qquad$ but now, I do, and I beg pardon of our congress of good people,
my powerful peers, my equally unfortunates, my narrow, callow fellows.

Allow me to tread the busy boulevards of our cities and the fencepost-
and-barbed-wire lanes of our countryside and the barely beaten paths
of our wilderness, released on my own recognizance to demonstrate

only who I am, as today, and more momentously, tomorrow, I live
my lengthening days to redeem that drab multitude of poor decisions
$\qquad\qquad$ made before the huddled wiser masses of the men I will become.

Yet Another Dream of Gary Snyder

52

Unpredictably—this *is* a dream, after all—the setting was a zendo,
a structure of golden wood, pitched beams, high windows open
to sky, breezes, and other inspirations, and not just any zendo—

    if you know what I mean—the *Ring of Bone* Zendo,
   which, of course, is located on Gary's land surrounded
by pines and firs and green sunlight and named after Lew's poem

    because—you know. That one time I spent the night
at Snyder's place, a little brown bat, which is likely the exact name
  of this tiny common creature, wove the shadows overhead

when the poet opened the door to sacred space, pointing to the floor
as a good place to unroll my sleeping bag in the dark. And I did.

I mean, who am *I* to argue with a famous poet? With my Eveready
   in one palm and everything else I grasp in the other, I kicked

the roll, and the shapeless fabric unspooled like thoughts in sleep.
As the bat peeped and flounced in the darkness I made by killing
the light, I lay me down to sleep. So there I am, snoozing in a zendo

with a bat aflit in the rafters—ironic, right? Yet that is *not* the night
I dreamed; *this* dream was last night, decades, a score of years later,

   on an island far from California. So today, before the dawn
most recent, I reposed again in that zendo, which in my nocturnal

imagination had broadened and deepened to an infinite space
of long tables and benches and many of my fellow humans eating

and drinking together as we do in shelters and mead halls
and centers of community everywhere. And, yes, as I expect
in my dreams about the man, Snyder was there, but I was surprised,

not about his presence in the hall or my dream, but that as we stood
beside the gleaming wall near the board of victuals, to me, the poet

whispered—not a volume expected of we who speak for a living—
    that I should now start giving more bread to the hungry

by carrying loaves to the tables and splitting the fresh and new
    with my hands and passing that essential steaming fare

to everyone without. I was not to worry, he advised, waving
    at the basket of bread, since no matter how often

I went to gather more, always more loaves would be stacked
    when I returned, and I did go back, and again, many times,
always denying the impulse to count the new loaves or to glance

    into the rafters at the bat navigating drafty shadows
beneath the ceiling beneath the sky. Snyder returned—I assume—

    to the kitchen where the real work of baking and stirring
and boiling and cutting occurs, and I—as directed by the poet—
paced the narrow aisles between the scraping of plates, clinking

of utensils, and thunking of cups while I awkwardly allotted
what's needed to all in need, knowing, as you do, we all discover
    that *is* the duty fallen to us. And I never once looked up

from the task, mindful, I suppose, that since life is ever seeking,
the little brown bat, too, found one way or another into the night
                   or the light.

Eric Paul Shaffer

A Lasting Mark, Dark and Greasy,
on the Ballcap of American Literature

for Gerardo

In Kailua, I sit at a table in the garage, folding clothes, oiling tools
and machines, measuring fertilizer one gloved handful at a time,
       busy at some task anyway. When eternity comes to mind,
there is no need to measure even a minute. I simply cannot
remember Friday, January 4, 1946, because I was yet to be born,
and I will recall exactly the same on Thursday, October 23, 2053.

    Still, I do recall gazing up at a red-tailed hawk and seeing
for the first time the grim pink sunlight forces through blood
       and feathers, but I have forgotten who stood near,
and I'm glad. In later years, with friends now gone, I lay on cool
    black lava in a good night, tracing with a green laser pointer,

the tail and fins of Delphinus, the smallest constellation, a dolphin
       back-flipping from the Milky Way. And I once feverishly
copied a sentence to quote from a friend's letter, and in the ruins
      of that hope, realized my friend was quoting *me*.

The finest pitch of the past is those days are done, glossed,
polished with loss. The sun today, broad and brilliant, reveals all.

Too much of the world is immaculate of me, but my passage
will surely damage driveways, snap limbs, or crush a bug. Bald
as I am, when I go, I wear a cap, sporting faded logos, but not even I

      care. On this table, left us by others we loved
now gone, with my little black dog at my feet, I fix this or break that,
    as trade winds mumble through palm fronds and the abiding

grind of a neighbor's washing machine. Such din glibly combines in my ears as silence, ephemeral and eternal. What a fucking glory is this life. May we all love all we can as long as we can.

The Purple Earth

for my beloved

Before there was enough oxygen for animals like you
and me to breathe, the world was dimmed in a thin scrim
        of CO_2 and methane, but that was then. And then,
hypothesize the scientists, the plants in ages we never knew
empurpled the world. Some would probably prefer to populate
        such a planet, a world with a hue royal and rare,
but since leaving this one will be the death of me, I'll stay
here at the red edge with you and luxuriate in the waste
        of oxygen in my every breath.

A Yearning for Misspelling

I, like you, want "eight" to be "right." And for me, too, "two"
and "too" have the saintly affinity of twins who differ too little
to be told apart. I want "spatial" to be "special," even sacred,

in the same way we love the land where we live. I see "their"
belongings belong "there" because those belong to, and next to,
them. And when "they're" is "there," I understand the explicit

distance between us and them, but I cannot forget that "here"
is also implicit in "there." And when I get "there," I see little

difference in "farther" and "further," for both name the same
place. I understand that going "boldly" requires the same fierce
courage as going "baldly" forth into the unknown, no matter rain

or shine. I know one might be cautious about how ineradicably
distinct each of us is from each, so "discreetly" and "discretely"
I sympathize without qualification with misspelling, and I share

that desire hidden deep within laziness and inattention, a refusal
to retrace the inky steps of composition. I want to except "accept"

as my sole and normal course and accept "except" as the odd
quantity and outlier I see at the heart of the word and the world.
And more than anything else I've ever read, right now, I want

"Steller's Jay" to be "Stellar's Jay," just for the heady, heavenly
intimation that indigo and midnight wings among the dark limbs
above our heads connect with the stars that hover even higher.

When I Can No Longer Stand What Is Broken

When I can no longer stand what is broken, I stop reading
         and sweep the pieces from the table to the tiles,
to carpet, to boards where a dustpan and brush will push
into a tidy pile grim shards that no longer inspire sense

         in any sense, no sense like the whole vase or mug
or loaf or book makes. I am disturbed by poetry dis-
composed in inexact pieces, like a bag of buttons or one
more hideous, broke-down, beat-up, rusted-out, done-in
car speeding the freeway on four of the "utility wheels"
the slick, smirking manufacturers now dump in trunks
as spares. Where do drivers ever find four such sad thin
rubber rims for the heedless highway? At the junkyard?
On an interstate median? In an alley behind Main Street
with tin cans and a spangle of crushed glass on oily earth?

All the broken lines undo what must be done. Limping
across a page without a subject. A single, simple verb
         with nothing doing. These fragments are the true
shore of our ruin, roaring, hissing, waves breaking what is
hard, solid, substantial, and essential by bashing boulders
into stones, into sand streaming like the force fracturing
         infinite and infinitesimal bits from beginnings born

in fire. Such words become sterile, disconnected dunes,
         piled and plied by the urgent, edgy elements of air
and water whose mutual work is, at best, only entropic

         and, at worst, as tenuous as the link between acting
and the curt, fleet state of the present, which flies

         as furiously into the future as the past pursues us.

Home Truths

"Home is the place where, when you have to go there,
They have to take you in."
—Robert Frost

"Home is where you hang your head."
—Groucho Marx

"There's no place like home."
—Dorothy

Instead of Writing Poems Today

I am washing dishes. I am making ice cubes, though the freezer
is full. I am gazing through a window at a mountain and a palm
tree I should be writing about. I am clearing my desk of junk

mail. I am considering the chaos of the wind chimes outside
my window, which to me makes glorious sense of the breeze.
I am answering correspondence, which is a tiresome parent to me,

demanding, unreasonable, inscrutable, and yet one whom I love
and hate even as I open each missive. I am petting the gray cat,
who mews once with each stroke of my palm. I am glancing

at the face of the clock, which, as I expected, is as blank
as my own face is. I am reading poems by poets whose work
delivers neither motive nor meaning in long lines of empty ink

and turning in fury to poets whose work eases me and shines
with clarity that seems beyond me. I am contemplating my box
of twenty-four Crayola crayons, particularly the one labeled

"dandelion/ diente de leon/ pissenlit," the first two of which do
indeed mean "tooth of the lion" and the last of which, fortunately,
does not mean "a leak on literature," but instead and surprisingly,

means "pee in bed." And now, I am contemplating a crayon
matching the neon childhood humiliation of stained bed sheets.
I am listening to my neighbors argue about something else

that annoys each about the other, words loud enough to hear
but too faint to follow. I am pondering the translation of a poem
by Cold Mountain, which I have framed and hung on the wall

nearby to distract me from my work. I am waiting for the wild
whoop of a car alarm to cease, wishing someone would just steal
the damned thing. I am watching sunlight spangle the leaves

of the mango tree, for which I am sure the exact Crayola color
is "green/ verde/ vert" though no shade matches the brilliance
of the ripening fruit. I am worrying about that clicking I heard

from the car's left rear wheel. I am watching my other neighbors
erect a picnic canopy in their yard as the fumigators tent the house
for termites. I am examining my fingers poised, restless and resting

on the keyboard, remembering my mother one long-ago day raising
both of them before our eyes and telling me my hands are beautiful.

King Tide

65

for my brother

The water of the swamp is clear, a little salty as an estuary
            always is, and I see the grass a few inches below
the rippled surface, green as summer as every blade gathers
                light. Today, the moon passes between Sol
        and Earth, the darkest face in the closest embrace.

And the gravity of this moment joins the sun to lift salt
from the sea into the sweet water flowing from the marsh
            at my feet. Not every day is a royal one, but this rise
                makes way for summer. And because of all
the dinosaurs still in the world, birds are the most beautiful,

I watch over the sodden lawn an ʻalae ʻula tread delicately
the water-covered grass. Just one. Silent, but for a modest
call. Just one. Yet bold in the light of today, gold feet pace
            the flood with the confidence of life that goes on
until there is no more. This dark bird bears fire like a secret,

a gift to us all. Such a tide does not happen every day,
                yet we see the hour coming, and we expect
what we can predict: a tide for a king. Here, water rises
in a rare surge, cresting all the shores we think we know

The Poor Box

My mother called it the poor box, a scarred square with a lock
of brass hung from a tongue-and-latch hinge. The silver of steel

shone through scratches in white paint. We paused near the box
as she dipped fingers in a basin and made a sign of the cross,
the same cross adorned by the bloody man hung above the pews.

Behind red glass on the altar was a flame to recall the presence
of God. I yearned to peek. Everything beneath the vaulted roof

enclosed mystery as the church enclosed us, under rough beams
lofty enough to cover the promises. The church was silent,
and the rows were empty. My mother chose the last and knelt.

I knelt, passing my time gazing at windows glowing red, green,
blue, and gold with glory and adoration. Dull daylight beyond
the windows animated the gem-colored tales on the stained glass.

In the station adorning the nearby wall was a thoughtless boy
in a busy market, ignoring a beaten man fallen beneath a cross.
When I returned later and alone, I dared not approach the flame

behind the rail, so I crept to the slotted lid. When I pried open
the battered box, the dented metal square contained only coins.

Self-Portrait at Birth

I screeched into the world like a pilot landing at Otis Air Force Base,
according to my mother, plopping into the black hands of the only

doctor on base willing to attend such silly events. I arrived early,
days before my ETA, touching down on the far side of the Atlantic

from the tiny town in Scotland, where during nocturnal explorations,
I was enthusiastically thumped into existence on a honeymoon

for the two virgins who became my astounded parents. My head
        was as long as a watermelon, and my mother was horrified

until the doctor squeezed my skull into a shape vaguely resembling
human, lop-siding my features into a face only a lover could love.

Fortunately, none looked closely at my squalling, wrinkled features
then, and few have done so since, so with my plain, unoriginal face—

a chimera captured by Kodak only once on film of black and white—
I stared blankly and baldly at a world witnessing my birth without

        applause, politely ignoring my every last leap into the air
since I first found my feet and launched into blue, clicking heels,

clapping hands, roughly, witlessly, relentlessly returning to Earth.

The Life and Death of Somebody's Son

By the riverbank, I spent the summer in the shade, pawing
          your thighs for gold, a teen forty-niner humped
over a secluded stream. You giggled on scratchy blankets,

          making me sweat and swear I'd write six songs
just for you. I bought beer with fake ID and a face looking
          older than I feel now for a picnic you called

"an orgy of bestiality"—breasts, thighs, legs—tonguing them
          obscenely as you grinned. We swallowed
every bite with a salt of sand braced by the bite of beer.

          We drank to tears until the day you cried,
said the baby was mine, your belly swelling with our son.
          But when I called, someone said you'd gone,

and hung up. I left the receiver dangling in the booth,
          limping down the middle of Main Street,
swearing I'd find you until sally or cindy or sandy someone.

          This morning, years later, you park a faded blue,
bumperless '68 VW Bug by a rural roadside, selling green
          and yellow vegetables you grow somewhere

in the woods with jimmie or timmie or tom. I hear our son
          was stillborn, and I dream his body bobs in a jar
on your kitchen windowsill among ripening tomatoes,

tooth-picked avocadoes, and stained-glass butterflies.

And This Is for You

When I found your grave, the stone was hidden in leaves
and thin drifts of cut grass. The lawn had crept over marble
       edges to crowd your name with green. I did not speak.

There was nothing to say. But I did kneel, and with my bare
hands, I brushed away leaves and litter and polished the stone
with a sleeve. I tore grass from the ground around the marble
until the dirt made dark moons of my fingernails. I played

       with the pinwheel I bought at a pharmacy downtown,
glossy scarlet and silver wings folded over deep interior blue.
With my breath, I whirled the blades faster than I could see.

       In this cemetery, the headstones are in the ground, level
with the earth. In this park of lawns and trees and trim roads,
we walk the world or do not. Rules are posted at the gates:
no memorials above ground. Visitors must leave no plants

or wreaths or flowers or flags or offerings. Our mementos
will be gathered and trashed so the mowers may freely shear
the grass on the graves to an even green. I sat on the ground

and watched a hawk glide low over the lawn and beat his way
back to the sky. Overhead, I heard a hummingbird and traffic
       on crossing freeways to the east, and I used a stick
to clean mud from the first few letters of your name. Yet

when I rose, I jammed the toy into the earth by your headstone
       and watched the wheel start to turn before I turned away.
The vanes glittered in the morning sun. When I looked back,

the only ghost was wind spinning the wheel. Let all
the groundskeepers curse me when they halt their machines
to rip those wings from the ground. Such remembrance is not
for you, nor is this cheap toy for them. This memorial is for me.

My Old Football Injury

My old football injury was done young.
        I was the center of the defensive line,
and I knew little of the game but hitting.
In the last play of my little career, I landed
on my side as the runner charged through.
        One foot lodged south of my calf
the other north of my thigh, and the scissors
of his all-out, full-tilt, goal-post run snapped
my knee backwards, opposite the common
course of flexion. My vision went blank,
and I heard nothing of my scream
        but the white noise of the cosmos.

Forty-five years later, today, I run as I do
        every day, to keep the knee loose,
the muscles around the joint tight. I run
        as far as I can to keep as long as I can
my straight pace and even gait, but limbering
the knee means I must march a hundred yards
after I run. Breathing hard, raising each leg high,
        back and forth in front of the house,
I make an absurd one-man parade of myself.

Giggling kids across the street snort and point,
fingers clutching a chain-link fence, watching
        this old man, marching, sweating in shorts
and a muscle T, as though as worthy as an athlete
        or someone famous. I understand the shrill
laughter and forgive their sport, for I know I lead

these boys as witlessly as a half-time drum major
to their own injuries in coming days when they take
        the field to play our silly, desperate games.

72

Angry at the Wind

My mother was angry at the wind for tearing clothes from the line,
for driving rain through open windows to soak beds and rugs,

for coating couches, lamps, coffee table, and dressers with a film
of dust. She was angry at the wind for slamming doors and banging
shutters, for flinging shingles from the roof and mounding leaves

        against the kitchen door. And she was angry at the wind
for carrying my father's words to her, as I, too, often did. She stood

in yellow sunshine, in a blue cotton dress, a scarf knotted beneath
unruly caramel curls. Back to the house, with sheets billowing,
        pegged shirts ballooning and inflated sleeves waving

        with elemental inspiration from the blue, she grimly hung
our costumes of those years, cleansed of a week of dirt and stain
and sweat. When I told her what my father had said, the wind

stole my words, and I will swear she never heard. Wooden clothes-
pins clamped in her teeth, she glared at a day that would not end,

        the wash that would never be done, and the relentless
sunshine and the swaying boles and lashing branches of green
        and gray drawing the wind for miles into a woods she wished

was a forsaken wilderness, a scatter of trackless shadows beyond
        our fence posts and wire, for her to enter and disappear.

Wedding Photo: September 8, 1954

South Ruislip, England

Smiling on the church sidewalk,
          my parents pose for posterity,
he slender and grinning, like a brat

from West Virginia, his hands firm
on her waist as she enters the taxi,

she, in a trim, sensible, white gown,
a prudent bouquet, and a modest
lace veil tucked behind her. I stare

into the pale, pure square that borders
their black-and-white beginnings,

her hidden foot raised for a small step
into eternity, that boxy, black cab,
          the driver invisible within,

only he ready, poised for the future,
          the wheel gripped in his fists,

in a vehicle that will carry them here
into my hands, now, before my eyes,
one moment cropped from the rest

when their happiness was perfect,
fixed in that last, immaculate instant

of possibility, with promises made,
yet unpaid, on a glad, gray day before
the same blank box framed me, too.

The Eleventh Street Irregulars

On any temporary sunny day in the valley, none of us had much
money, but my friends complained about the cheap beer I bought,
        the Lucky Lager, the Old Milwaukee, the PBR,
but still I filled the rusted fridge with cans and brown bottles.

"Life's too short for cheap beer," one gazing into the lightless chill
        would growl, but we knew better and cracked another.
        The sun was going down, and we knew that, too.

        From the street's dead end, slumped on the couch, tired
after long afternoons restoring the decrepit boat, we watched trains
        pass and deciphered riddles in bottle caps we twisted free
        with empty hands and our ready, useless strength.

        Nobody loved my car, either, a used Plymouth Champ
of babysplat brown graced with a sporty, black stripe and an engine
        that ran and ran and ran. My mother gave me,

gave me, that car, as she gave me the life I was happily wasting.
She knew I had no wheels and thought I might eventually
        need to get somewhere. My friends found that car—
with inexplicably pulsing combustion, in a cadence like breathing,

lacking in cool or charm, useful only in an emergency, a task,
or a chore. Or sometimes, the car was amusing, as on the morning,
        after driving one of us downtown for court, I stopped

at a traffic light beside a police car. The Champ, panting
        at the pause, suddenly sounded its horn, announcing,
in a way I never could, "Hey, I'm here!" When the cop, inscrutable
        behind dark lenses, turned, I raised my hands to the sky

in the universal gesture of *I have no idea.* His badge glinted
as he chuckled. The light changed, and, shaking his head, the law
drove on into another life, and with a sigh of relief, so did I.

On long evenings, our dogs slept at our feet, and the boat gleamed
pale beneath a tree someone planted decades ago for future shade.
Keel to the stars, raised on sawhorses, the hull was sanded, ready
   for paint, misadventure, and the Sacramento. Like all men

of no particular use, looking for work and finding only jobs,
we spent time and money passing time and spending money,
   and told the stories at dusk, sitting on the couch, the porch,

or the steps, laughing as loudly and often as the tale demanded.
   Life, we decided, was good, or at least, remarkably better
     than the alternative. There was, after all, the river
and a boat to restore and someday launch onto the muddy flow.

So we spent our days and dollars together, and no matter what else,
   there was always beer to drink, and a car to borrow,
    or a ride to a place we needed to go.

Surrounded by Sky

The neighborhood I left when I was nine
left with me, packed in cardboard boxes
stacked with carpets and scarred furniture
we should have sold. The bricks and eaves
and maples and oaks were gone for good

once we headed west from Mussula Road
in an extravagant series of turns that led
to where I am now, far from those blazing
days of infinite minutes and narrow streets

on the maps of places I will never see again.
As we, and then I, traveled, days grew short,
minutes measured, and seasons were a flash
of sun or snow. No more were the mornings
when my father bent to lift me from the grass

into the dawn above his head and toss me high.
I know now I was never as young as my father
was then, in corduroy and shirtsleeves, strong
scents of tobacco and Old Spice, tall and trim
before the house in a yard of morning with me

held above his head and then thrown upward
from his muscled arms, away from the sullen
earth, rising yet into the light and consummate
blue, arms open, laughing, surrounded by sky.

The Glazier

One of my ancestors, I imagine, was a glazier,
framing stained glass windows for a cathedral in a century
of construction in some shadow in a Europe benighted
by plagues and priests. The lead from the work worked

well into his blood and his brain before he reached
the narrow, desperate day when he would complete a pane
or an entire window depicting an angel or a disciple, a saint,
a throne, or a dove, and then smash the scene with a mallet

crowned with a dull head of iron, dented, scratched
with years of harder blows. Then, he would gather more
sharp, brilliant shards, lead the edges, and start another hard
lurid scene of passion or salvation to shatter in the next dark

tomorrow, now centuries ago. All I wonder is why.
Was this bent, dirty man saving his daily bread by destroying
his work? Was this obliteration his grim dismissal of faith?
Was he announcing his dissatisfaction with the art

he practiced without perfection? Was he acting religiously
on his conviction he was not worthy to illustrate God
and the heavens he created? I see him, staring into the fire
as the brittle bits melted, considering creation and damnation,

squatting among chickens, pigs, and children
in the muddy yard at dawn as glass cools enough for tinting,
for the sweet, hot, poisonous lead, for the piecing of slivers
into brittle images illuminated by the light beyond the glass.

Parsley

I was a small boy sitting beside my mother at the lunch counter
on a spinny, round red stool at Reed's Drugstore. My hamburger
arrived on one of those gloriously thick, heavy, white plates

scoured so thoroughly and often that the glaze had worn away.
The edges dulled and lost their finish first. My mother wore a hat,
lipstick, and smoked while I ate. There was a soda fountain,

and the menu listed malts, banana splits, root beer floats.
Baltimore was pleasantly unhurried on the avenues and boulevards

of the suburbs. In the parking lot beyond the plate glass
were florid fins, hefty fenders, and chrome detailing every arc,
crease, and corner of varnished wood and vulcanized rubber.

Every polished, blinding, silver bumper was good American steel.

The world was tipping a bit, and my mother could feel the tilt.
The smell of fresh roasted Spanish peanuts was in the air,
hot, salty, and bronze in their skins. Near the edge of my plate

was a thin green sprig of limbs my mother told me was parsley.
"Don't eat that. It's just there for color." Behind a sugar bowl

and shakers of pepper and salt, pie was displayed in a glass case:
apple, blueberry, or cherry. A ring within was bent, and the circular
symmetry intended in the design was gone. She smoked.

Ashtrays shone on the Formica countertop, unscratched, unstained,
and limitless. As I ate, I questioned the purpose
of parsley in a world buzzing with more colors than I could name.

Joe Dickie's Last Hallowe'en

The last time I saw my father, he was dressed
as George Washington, wearing the grand, white curls
of a powdered wig, a broad, black belt, with knee socks

and polished, silver-buckled shoes. His greatcoat
was red, white, and blue, a blue the same faded shade

as sky. The white had weathered to gold, but the red
was right. He carried a thick D.C. phone directory
he had covered with a brown grocery bag as I once did

my schoolbooks. With Magic Marker, he had lettered
the cover with the legend USS *Constitution*.
I didn't bother to correct him. I just watched him walk

into the windy darkness of sidewalks and bare branches
with an empty pillowcase swinging from his other hand.

Scabs and Other Childhood Lies

82

Even as I slumped in the stained-glass stupefaction
of church on a Sunday morning, I couldn't blame
my parents. When they spoke of Jesus and heaven,
the story glowed in their eyes. The words were dull

knives inching stitches through gristle in cheap meat
served with our bread and beans at the dinner table.
All the grief in faith arises from that milled knot
of paradox, shellacked in planks beneath our plates,

when what should have become a branch offering
leaves to light becomes a hard eye staring at the dark.
But I could not forgive the lies about Santa Claus,
the Easter Bunny, and Yahtzee. And even worse,

they smiled and lied again about the Tooth Fairy
while I cowered before my vision of pale loops
in a loose necklace strung with polished baby teeth
clicking hungrily as she leaned through my sleep

to slide a quarter beneath my snot-stained pillow.
And those were the silver decades when a quarter
dropped to the sidewalk rang like a bell of wealth.
Lies of many colors shone in the red and blue

and green and gold glass between me and the day
I craved. Yes, Santa will bring toys to the good
girls and boys. Yes, Nana is in heaven now. Yes,
you'll win the game when you shake the dice

long enough and scatter the bones far and wide
enough for God to tip the dark spots toward luck.
Yes, that is a monster in the closet. Yes, I love
you. Yes, I'll be here today when you get home.

The worst lie was that everything will be all better.
Someone would sigh, "There, it's all better now,"
after a hiss of Bactine or the crackle of a Band-Aid
or a sloppy kiss on the owie. That lie *is* a lie, a lie

amazing in the same way sunlight on pretty pink flesh
gleams on a knee after a scab falls, a fierce beacon
blazing with promise, before burning brown in long
summer light, and then, that new skin tears away, too.

Orphaned at Sixty

I'm so old sixty still sounds like a speed limit to me.
        My orphaning started long ago, for the man
who claimed he was my father died long before

                the man who said he was not my father,
even though both looked like the same man. The limits
        were roadside signs he ignored. He drove

half-asleep, with the whole family wide-awake
                and watching, crying when tires crossed
        the centerline or dropped from the roadway

to the shoulder. The miles disappeared beneath
                heavy lids and a heavy foot. Nobody slept
but the driver. Anyway, the keys are mine now,

        and the world is emptier and bigger and fuller
and brighter and, some say, flatter. With no father
to obscure my vision, the planet rolls open to my eyes,

        so if the horizon is not the edge of the world,
somebody say so, because with miles rolling beneath me,
        I'm awake, watching, approaching the imminent.

Cigarettes in Paradise

Visiting my mother's grave was much easier before my father
moved in. I could sit on the grass or snow and speak my mind
to her boxed bones two fathoms down, but now his ashes come
between us. Some words, I want to say only to her, but the urn

containing his incinerated body intercepts what my mother and I
have shared without him for the twenty-nine years she's passed
in the peace of carefully-tended desert beneath the concrete
interchange of I-40 and I-25. I used to tell her about the hawks

and hummingbirds I spied as mowers drew monotonous lines
through the grass and trucks down-shifted overhead, and I left
a carton on her marble marker. Now when we talk, I only see
the two of them, distracted, she strutting the gold-plated streets

between pink marble villas in Paradise, wishing for a cigarette,
and he crooked in her arm in a ribbed green 32-ounce coffee can.
His voice reverberates from aluminum emptiness as they argue,
increasingly impatiently, how they should spend all of eternity.

She glances down the silver side streets, wondering where the hell
the 7-Eleven is anyway. If this is heaven, where is the celebratory
smoke they deserve? We all know from our antics on this planet
we should never ask for what we deserve, but maybe when we die,

we just get what we expect, God, demons, karma, a grand design.
The Mormons get their presidency, personal planet, and slaves.
The Muslims get their seventy-two virgins or ... white raisins.
The Christians get to chortle, hoot, and shout from the balcony,

gloating over the sufferings of all they *knew* were going to Hell.
The Hindus get another turn, and Buddhists get to skip every turn
for eternity. The snake-handlers get snakes; Wiccans get oaks,
robes, and Stonehenge; the Scientologists get aliens. Quakers get

white light. I get the big nothing I always anticipated. Best of all,
if we get what we expect, none of "those *awful* people" will enter
our exclusive, gated Elysian Estates; we alone will select the wives,
children, and friends who attend us. As my parents wander through

rose and golden light under pale purple clouds, I'm sure my mother
sometimes shakes the half-empty can as my father hisses within.
Her glorious laugh will spark their running joke as she reminds him,
"You're fired." And even as I blab away below, live from Earth,

about my mortal tribulations and triumphs, my mother will locate
the well-stocked white, chrome, and glass convenience she seeks,
accept her pack of Merit (regular), and light up. The rising smoke
of her satisfaction will add perfection to the endless, ethereal blue.

Hiking the Fire Access Road

for Mariah Blackhorse

Gravel graces two tracks worn through wildflowers and grass gone seedy,
and all of this is for fire. If this road through the woods leads anywhere,
we'll never use it to get there. Not today. Not tomorrow. We've walked

farther than daylight and canteens allow. Silence around us deepens
to the proper hue. Twilit trees are slow explosions uncoiling from soil.

Where the ground is scorched, the walking is easy. The soil is ash,
and the seeds and spores germinating there are something we wish

we understood but never will. There's little use trying. Such trails are
promises to the present of which the future makes the most. We trace

tracks gouged from the ground while fecundity runs an inexplicable course
around us, through us, beyond us. We know little more of that blind urge
than it terrifies and trivializes us into exaggerations we call fear and hope.

The simple impulse to press progeny into existence is a wildfire within
us, whether they like it, or we like it, or not. Surge and spasm is all.

Mushrooms rise from the dirt as trees do. Moss blooms. Lichen grows.
Deer mate and die by the hunter's gun and the snapped ankle. We follow

the curve around the hill, a slope of a million years. Bones and limbs litter
the way. The fire in the forest is beyond our control. The stars reclaim

the sky, and no matter how bleak or bright the moon, light draws the eye.
We stumble through a night new to us. Our noisy passage scatters seeds,
and some believe we serve a purpose, but none can ever know or choose.

What My Brother Might Say as a River

My voice is a rush of white over rocks stacked by the current
on my tongue. The passage I've cut for myself through the firs,

      spruce, and hemlock is too narrow for my language.
The water of which I am made is not what I am: I am the place
I pass, the one where you meet me, and I depart even as I arrive

where you stand. I am a gathering of storms, of rain and clouds.
I am the cascade that passes, carrying what is and covering

what is not. I bear cold from peaks to the plains the sun rules.
If I change, I change slowly or swiftly, under the direction

      of seasons and stars. I am one flow, yet stones break

my way into many courses. I seek the sea in the thrill of descent,
and I yearn to enter something larger than myself. I turn aside

travelers and paths, and my presence demands bridges and boats,
fords and fishers. Silence is the essence of my surge, yet I am

      the last place one seeks peace, for I enforce the solitude

of high places. I have no more to say than the rain, frost, or snow,
the fog or the sea. I give myself only to those creatures who bow.

You Little Bastards

When I tell my wife my mother called her children "little bastards,"
she is surprised. At first, I really don't know why. I thought all
mothers called their children "little bastards." Apparently not. I knew
my mother longest, not best, of her sons and daughters, but I can't claim
to have been the spawn she loved most, and I certainly irked her enough

to recall anger as much as affection. She simply called us, mad or not,
"You little bastards." She would say, "You little bastards, get in the car."
Or "You little bastards better stop fighting before your father comes home."
Or "Come on, you little bastards, the turkey's on the table." If a bastard
is a child born out of wedlock, then, as far as I know, we weren't truly

bastards. Papers and pictures suggest my parents were married,
and they wore the gold links on their fingers as proof. And if Jesus was
the bastard son of Mary and the Almighty, I suppose I'm also a bastard

in that exquisite sense: someone amazing who came from nowhere,
much to the annoyance of all. And my mother prepared me well for the end.

Now, when whoever comes to lead us dead into darkness commands me
to the wrong side of the grass, I'll go quick. As I kneel on the bare, muddy
banks of Lethe, dipping my Dixie cup into the rainbowed and smoking
black waters, I'll be ready, even comforted, when the angry ferryman
yells into the vaulted cavern above the weeping faces of my companions,

"Come on! Drink up! Hurry! Let's go, you little bastards!"

And Now, After **Second Nature**

Why Second Nature, *or How Much Nature Can One Contain?*

Here we are. For those of you who wonder, and I am guessing that's you, *second nature* is a phrase, foreign and familiar from the longitudes and latitudes of the landscapes of language. Earlier in the book, I, well, actually, at my urging, Jordan, my exalted and stellar publisher, placed the phrase "a practice natural enough to look natural." What looks natural is done with an economy of motion that pleases the eye, the mind, and the heart. Pretty much, that's all, but far be the day from me that I ever let a few words do the work when I have so many.

So, yes, any action enacted well will look easy. *Practice*, however, contains the perfect double-meaning. *Practice*, doing something over and again to learn the best way to do that something, and *practice*, doing something because that is just what one does, are two and the same meaning. *Practice* makes an action better and is exactly what one does—simultaneously—the same action accomplishes both goals. Even more, regular and repeated action refines action even more. *Practice* is what you do, what you always do, and what refines what you do. The goal of *practice* is not to create an identical result, but to achieve the same goal. I don't want to write the same poem over and over again; I want to write a different good poem over and over again. May these lines, therefore, demonstrate and celebrate *second nature.*

Second nature is a state of the universe one enters where all is changed, yet all remains the same with a little more grace, balance, and poise in the elegant moment of action, a state in which the quality of daily existence is transformed, where the moment encompasses each of us fully, and the past and future trouble us no more because neither exists as neither has always not existed. *Second nature* opens a new universe for each to enter and inhabit fully the parameters of the moment. *Second nature* is the state in which the Venn diagram of two circles, one circle for "I" (whatever one means when one says "I") and another circle for the universe, fully and completely overlap. In *second nature*, all of the above merges, and here we are.

Second Nature is what I hope these poems convey. In other words, these lines present, present again, or re-present observations of the world, the planet, and myself for your delectation, amusement, and, as Rod might say, your approval. This is just to say, my fellow apes and Terrans, there's nature, the one we all mean when we say "nature," and then, there's *second* nature, meaning my, your, and our versions of the original, upon which agreement is prospective and provisional. I offer these lines to help you make up your mind.

The Ideal Edition of Second Nature, *or Any Book of Poems*

A volume of poems is basically a list, one poem after another. To include all, an order is unavoidable. Still, readers have two ways to proceed. First, open the book randomly and read whatever the page and eye discover; gather, rinse, and reread as necessary. Such is my preferred method for books of mine and others. Or, second, open the book to the first poem, then read the next, then read the next, then read the next until you complete each section and every poem.

I prefer the first method. My ideal edition of a book of poems arrives on two CDs — remember those? — CD #1 contains all of the poems included in the book, each with a single, separate track, and the CD is programmed to present the poems simply, frankly, and only randomly. That's right: sequence in a book of poems is, thus, not only ideally ignored, but positively denied. Every time a reader begins, a new order of the pages is manifest, a destiny, declaration, and demonstration devoutly to be wished. Any one of the sixty poems included here may appear first or last or in-betweeny. The random puts the lines on the line. Can every poem bear such weight, such stress, such fortuitousitude /FOR-two-ih-TIS-uh-TOOD/? Will what precedes and succeeds any one work and work well? Well, let's see now. Lock in that shiny, silver plate and press "Play."

CD #2 would include this boring afterface and publication notes and ordering details and ISBNs and Library of Congress Numbers and acknowledgments and lists of my other works (and I do have some!) and the horrors of my biography set out in exacting, excruciating, and embarrassing detail. I advise never playing CD #2.

At the end of this book of poems whirling unexpectedly by, I would like readers to be a little shaken, unhinged even, stirred to action, ready for an exacting examination of exactly what each one of us is and what we are to each other. Once entered, I now pronounce *Second Nature* inescapable and everlasting, like a black hole, like the future, like a book of poems.

The Ones I Am Lucky Enough to Remember to Name

A long list of those I love: Veronica Winegarner. Jordan Jones. Derek Otsuji. Leslie Martin. Lisa Cadenas. James Taylor III. John Kain. Kathryn Capels. Melanie VanderTuin. Jordan Jones (a name so nice, I thank him twice). Matt Daly. José A. "Tony" Alcántara. Michael Blanchard. David and Jeannette Robertson. Ed Davis. Alice Hamilton. Amanda Hayden. Aimee Noel. As for the rest of you, you know what you did, I know your names, and I thank you. I here declare my gratitude for the fun and good lessons you taught me; I'll take those to the grave.

A Provisional Proviso for the Next Decade

In June, 2026, I will enter my eighth decade. I do, and maybe we all should, consider the likelihood of successive and remaining years baldly (check), boldly (double check), and closely (triple check), so here goes. I am certainly less likely to emerge from this decade, as defined by my birthly origins, than I was to pop from the second or fourth or sixth. According to good sources, in fact, I've already lived more than 90% of my life and daily approach my expected expiration date of seventy-six years. No more skipping dessert.

Meditations on slim mortality are good for us all, especially after Mr. Mojo Risin's excellent point about the unlikely possibility of escape, so I remain as cognizant as I have for years now of the good luck in every moment. Like you, I hope for many tomorrows, but I expect a few fewer these days.

Despite anonymous actuarial auspications (contemplate for a moment how many of my remaining minutes I spent flipping the pages of a dictionary to find that word!), I still *look forward to,* which means *hope for,* another ten to fifteen years at least, mainly to finish all of the books I've begun, so I already anticipate seeing you on the far side of eighty, trailing clouds of glorious publications. If I'm already gone, sorry I missed you. Please leave a message.

Good luck to us all.

Eric Paul Shaffer
February 1, 2026 / Kailua, O'ahu, Hawai'i

Notes

Photo on the dedication page: That is, indeed, my brother Joseph Arthur Shaffer (1956–2025) and I (1955–) posed in the living room of my grandmother Corrine Filander's house in Towson, Maryland. He is dressed as a scout of the Old West, and I'm garbed as a motorcycle police officer, affording an unexpected glimpse into our futures. Turning the photograph "over" reveals this inscription: "Dec. 29, 1960: Eric + Joey all dressed up in their Christmas outfits from 'Nana' Gates. They came to spend the night with 'Gram' so I took their picture when they arrived. They were so pleased for being dressed up—as you can see."

Field Trips: For once, events recounted in a poem really happened. From 1964 to 1969, my family lived at 7830 Valley Park Road in Peppermill Village in Seat Pleasant, Maryland, right at the eastern tip on the diamond of the District of Columbia. All my siblings and I were students at Carmody Hills Elementary School, and I attended fourth grade with Mrs. Mixa, fifth grade with Mrs. Chambers, and sixth grade with Miss Nichols. As a sixth-grader at Carmody Hills Elementary School, I spoke to Ethel Kennedy on the phone, shook the hand of Robert F. Kennedy in the Attorney General's Office, and held a $10,000 bill at the U.S. Mint, which stopped printing that denomination in 1969.

From my bedroom window, I really *could* see the dome of the U.S. Capitol and the Washington Monument, a fact that even then struck me as remarkable. While my family lived in Maryland, Robert F. Kennedy and Martin Luther King, Jr. were assassinated, and smoke from the fires burning on the lettered and numbered streets rose high over the suburbs.

One of my favorite parts of living near Washington, D.C., was the field trips, and my class took every one mentioned here.

The Creaking of the Net: Among the most renowned poets of ecology are Robinson Jeffers (1887–1962) and Gary Snyder (1930–). Jeffers was a fundamental and formative influence for Snyder. Jeffers and Snyder accord in their thinking and writings concerning the emergency that twentieth-century industry and commerce pose, and Snyder's *Turtle Island* sounded a call for a broader, deeper understanding of humanity and the planet. The work of both poets radiates disgust and deep frustration concerning human action devoted to destroying the planet. I allude to the image of the net in Jeffers' poem "The Purse-Seine."

That Girl on Fire: The first photograph may be the most well-known image of the Viet Nam War, and like all of the horrors of the '60s influenced me permanently. The second photograph punched me right in the heart with the revelation that much can still go right in the world. Both illustrate the way fire shapes us all, against our will and before our eyes. I am particularly grateful to Michael Blanchard who first published this poem in *Slant,* then invited me to his class to answer student questions about "one of those wars."

Traci's Sunset* and *Flappy: On October 8, 2016, Ashley Wellman drove a car broadside into a pickup truck at the approximate speed of 127 miles per hour, killing my sister-in-law Tracy Winegarner and her partner Debi Wylie. Ashley survived with only minor injuries. The decline of my parents-in-law Charles and Nance was hastened by the shock, and, stricken with Alzheimer's disease, both passed away in 2019. This pair of poems commemorates the lives of these two wonderful women I loved and miss every day.

My Balderdashery: This poem begins with Lew Welch. Somewhere in the novel, *I, Leo,* Lew spots a sign for "Leo's Haberdashery," which stuck in his mind because, born on August 16, Lew was a Leo, astrologically speaking, and the odd concurrence of the personal and zodiacal names led to adoption of the lion as one of his many avatars, until he learned better later. Meanwhile, the word *haberdashery* stuck in mine. A haberdashery was originally a shop selling small miscellaneous goods, especially sewing materials, and later became a name for a store selling men's apparel and accessories, especially hats. I always found amusing the idea of an emporium devoted exclusively to distributing articles in all sizes of what I consider male bullshit. The home office where I write, which I call "The Literature Factory," is a place where I create weird stuff, so the word *balderdashery* leaped to mind, and yes, I'm pretty sure I invented that word, too.

On another hand, Diogenes of Sinope, the famed fourth-century Cynic and ascetic Greek philosopher, reputedly lived outside under a tub. Depicted as rough of life and sharp of tongue, he was revered for clear assessment of the features and failings of human life. Hearing of Diogenes, Alexander the Great was impressed and sought out the man. When the two met, Alexander immediately demonstrated his misunderstanding of the philosophy of abnegation and freedom from possessions that Diogenes embodied. According to Plutarch (and if we can't trust Plutarch, who *can* we trust?), The Great offered the philosopher whatever in the world he wanted, pledging to grant that wish. Diogenes' reply: "Get out of my light." Amusingly, ever after, Alexander coveted the tub of Diogenes.

***On a Celebrated Cover of* APR:** During the nineteen-eighties I lived in Davis, California, and I was studying literature hard and trying harder to write some. To stay current with the world of poetry, I subscribed to poetry magazines, among those *American Poetry Review,* a newsprint tabloid. One month, probably between 1984 and 1987, the cover featured box after box of poets' faces, twenty or thirty visages stacked in rows and columns, and I was struck that whoever chose the photos picked the most unattractive shots. Sad, yet funny. (Let me know if you find the issue I'm talkin' 'bout.) By the way, in the years since, composers of poems, female and male, have grown, mysteriously, much more beautiful.

Exfinition: Art Goodtimes once asked me to elaborate on "exfinition," a word I coined casually during our correspondence concerning writing poetry. At the time, in direct opposition to the word *definition,* I meant the writerly attempt to free words from the confining bounds of denotation by pressing meaning to the limits of lexical endurance.

For years, the notion percolated between my ears, but blossomed when I was paired in an ekphrastic endeavor with painter Ernest Williamson III by editor Jenny O'Grady, as part of the mission of *the light ekphrastic* to generate more ekphrastic art by introducing artists of all types in order to encourage the creation of new works through mutual appreciation. I encourage all artists to join in that exhilarating project: thelightekphrastic.com. Our assignment was for me to write a poem responding to one of Ernest's paintings while he painted a work in response to one of my poems.

Ernest's painting entitled "Outside of Ourselves," a canvas of swirling curves and shifting colors, reminded me of my notion that even the most forceful of demarcations fade, wither, and wane. Additionally, Ernest's title for the painting recalled and reinforced the imaginary and arbitrary nature of nearly every line we draw among and between ourselves and the planet. And the title of the work became part of my poem's first line. To see the paintings and poems: thelightekphrastic. com/williamson-shaffer-november-2024.

Then, I remembered an art appreciation class: as I was led through the halls of London's Tate Gallery, the instructor Mr. Bradbury noted that many medieval landscape paintings depict a continuous view, often chopping elements of the scene arbitrarily at the edge of the canvas. To further press my luck and suggest the permeability of limits and lexicon, I slackened my typical rejection of fragments for use in poetry. Moreover, to celebrate the invented word of the title, I created more new words to include in the poem. How many can *you* find?

Eight Points at the Navajo Bunkhouse: The Navajo Bunkhouse was my assigned accommodation at the 2006 Fishtrap Writers Retreat and Workshop. I studied there with Luis Urrea, who gave us the good advice to take long afternoon walks to learn whatever we could directly from the planet. As far as I can tell, Enterprise, Oregon, is located within the territory of the Nez Perce, and far from the traditional territory of the Navajo Nation in Arizona, New Mexico, and Utah. I asked about the name, but got no answer. I remain perplexed.

Yet Another Dream of Gary Snyder: I don't know about you, but my dreams are spectacularly surprising to me. As narrator in my own dream, I am usually someone I have never been. In a smaller percentage, I am my plain old quotidian self in situations so strange I wouldn't tell you anything about the events if I could. I rarely dream about anyone I actually know, but Gary Snyder has appeared in my dreams ever since I met the man in 1984. In the new millennium, I began a project of using the dreams as starting points for poems, and this one, too, accurately recounts one night I spent at Kitkitdizze, flashlight, sleeping bag, and bat.

The Ring of Bone Zendo is a real and gorgeous meditation hall, whose name was chosen from Lew Welch's excellent poem, usually titled by the first line "[I saw myself]." The work of Welch is exemplary, so find and read Lew Welch's *Ring of Bone: Collected Poems*. "Song of the Turkey Buzzard," is, in my estimation, one of the greatest ecological poems of the twentieth century, lovingly influenced and inspired by Robinson Jeffers' poem "Vulture."

King Tide: "King Tide" commemorates the life of my brother Joseph Arthur Shaffer. From the times we were teens, my nickname for my brother was J.B., initials short for something I don't remember and won't share. This book is dedicated to him.

A King Tide, also known as a Royal Tide or Spring Tide, is one of the highest tides of the year, occurring only a few times annually, when the pull of the sun is accompanied by a full or new moon. The water swells higher when the moon is at perigee, the point of closest approach to Earth. These tides are natural and predictable but uncommon. I observed a King Tide in May 2025 while walking along the Kawainui, a freshwater marsh connected to the Pacific by a canal and estuary. On the day I learned of my brother's death, the tide rose over the grass on the streamside, and birds wandered through the water over the submerged green.

The 'alae 'ula is a native Hawaiian bird, a solitary walker often hard to find, not because the bird hides, but instead walks easily over open ground and within the abundance of green alongside the stream. The terrain, tangled or free, is all the same to this species. Endemic to the islands, the 'alae 'ula displays a bill and forehead shield of gleaming red, unusual for gallinule species, recalling that the bird is recognized as the bringer of fire in Hawaiian mythology. The 'alae 'ula stole fire from the god Maui, brought that blaze to the people, and was forever after marked with flame. The bird's solitary nature and habitation on the verge of water and land, at the merging of two elements, reminded and reminds me of my brother.

***And Now, After* Second Nature:** The famed Jim Morrison (1943–1971), singer, songwriter, and co-founder (with Ray Manzarek) of The Doors, created an anagram of his name: "Mr Mojo Risin," suggestive of sexual prowess and ascent. The name is repeated incrementally in volume as a line in the song "L.A. Woman." Jim appears here because of the early, unexpected death that made him a legend as well as the title of the Jerry Hopkins and Danny Sugerman biography, *No One Here Gets Out Alive,* a line taken from the song "Five to One," and as far as I can tell, truer every year.

Acknowledgments

Grateful acknowledgment is made to the editors of the following publications, in which these poems are forthcoming, first published, or reprinted.

The American Journal of Poetry: A June Afternoon with Michael

The Antigonish Review (Canada): Travel Notes on Bells in Japan

AZURE: A Journal of Literary Thought: My Balderdashery

Bamboo Ridge: Once, A Mango Tree; Perseid Meteor Shower, Oʻahu; Traci's Sunset; A Tree Newly Planted in the Islands at the Edge of the World

Central American Literary Review (Nicaragua): Wedding Photo: September 8, 1954

Chiron Review: Hiking the Fire Access Road

Cider Press Review: Traffic Accident on Main Street

Coastal Shelf: Traffic Accident on Main Street

Coe Review: The Life and Death of Somebody's Son

Confrontation: The Poor Box

Dancing at the Crossroads: Last Poems: 2010–2013 by Michael Adams: A June Afternoon with Michael

Deep Wild: Eight Points at the Navajo Bunkhouse

di-vêrsé-city Anthology: 2017 Austin International Poetry Festival: My Red Watch Cap

Fishtrap Anthology 2006: Becoming Native to Place: Eight Points at the Navajo Bunkhouse

The Frost Meadow Review: And This Is for You

Gargoyle: God as a Dispenser of Pez; On My Love, Losing Her Hearing; Yet Another Dream of Gary Snyder

Going Down Swinging (Australia): Cigarettes in Paradise

Grasslimb Journal: Angry at the Wind

Green Ink: Hiking the Fire Access Road

Halfway Down the Stairs: September 10, 2001; That Girl on Fire

Hawai'i Review: The Creaking of the Net; Dark Matters; You Little Bastards

The Hole in the Head Review: Orphaned at Sixty

Kestrel: Parsley

the light ekphrastic: Exfinition

LitBop: Scabs and Other Childhood Lies

Mad Blood: The Economy of Signs; Flappy

Magma (England): My Plea of Not Guilty

Main Street Rag: A Few Words for Jesus

The National Poetry Review: When I Can No Longer Stand What Is Broken

North American Review: A Lasting Mark, Dark and Greasy, On the Ballcap of American Literature; The Murder Weapon

The Pedestal Magazine: Angry at the Wind

The Poetry Lighthouse: The Purple Earth; Self-Portrait at Birth

Prole (Wales): Extremities

The Quadrant Magazine (Australia): Small Town Affairs; Steering into the Skid

Recasting Masculinity: An Anthology (The Beautiful Cadaver Project): My Old Football Injury

Rosebud: Top Ten Bumper Stickers for American Poets

SHINE Poetry Quarterly: King Tide

Slant: One for Sorrow; That Girl on Fire; The Glazier; The Ones Who Didn't Know

Solo: On Contemplating a Celebrated Cover of *APR*

SOUTH Poetry Magazine (England): Surrounded by Sky

Southword Journal (Ireland): Instead of Writing Poems Today

Spillway: Poet Lesson #53: How to Pick Up a Lover

The Stand Magazine (England): Field Trips; A Gift from a Collector; Joe Dickie's Last Hallowe'en; On Giving You the Shirt Off My Back; A Yearning for Misspelling

The Sun Magazine: The Eleventh Street Irregulars

Weber: The Contemporary West: A Blessing for Companions Who May Never Again Share a Table; Don't Mention It; What My Brother Might Say as a River

William and Mary Review: The Life and Death of Somebody's Son

About the Author

Eric Paul Shaffer is author of ten volumes of poetry, most recently *Green Leaves: Selected & New Poems* and *Free Speech*, both from Coyote Arts. More than 650 of his poems have been published in Australia, Canada, Costa Rica, England, Germany, India, Iran, Ireland, Japan, Netherlands, New Zealand, Nicaragua, Scotland, Singapore, Wales, and the United States. A few have been translated into Esperanto, Farsi, or Spanish. His work appears in twenty-seven anthologies, including *Fire and Rain: EcoPoetry of California* (Scarlet Tanager, 2018), *The EcoPoetry Anthology* (Trinity UP, 2013), *Jack London Is Dead: Contemporary Euro-American Poetry in Hawai'i* (Tinfish, 2013), *100 Poets Against the War* (Salt, 2003), and *The Soul Unearthed* (Tarcher/Putnam, 1996).

Shaffer's first novel *Burn & Learn, or Memoirs of the Cenozoic Era* was published in 2009. Other fiction appears in *Bakunin, Bamboo Ridge, Natural Bridge,* and *News from the Republic of Letters,* and in two chapbooks, *You Are Here* (2004) and *The Felony Stick* (2006).

Shaffer received Hawai'i's 2002 Elliot Cades Award for Literature to an established writer; Ka Palapala Po'okela Book Awards for *Lāhaina Noon* (2006) and *Even Further West* (2019); the 2009 James M. Vaughan Award for Poetry; Lorin Tarr Gill Writing Competition Awards (Poetry, first place, 2010; Nonfiction, first place, 2020; Poetry, third place, 2020). Shaffer received a poetry fellowship to attend the 2006 Summer Fishtrap Writers Workshop. In 2015, he was a visiting poetry faculty member at the 23rd Annual Jackson Hole Writers Conference in Wyoming, and has been a returning presenter, delivering the Keynote Address in 2013, at the Ko'olau Writers Workshops sponsored by Hawai'i Pacific University, a visiting poet and guest of the School of Language & Literature and *SLANT: A Journal of Poetry* at the University of Central Arkansas in 2024, and keynote speaker and presenter at The Poets' Roundtable of Arkansas, the state affiliate member of the National Federation of State Poetry Societies, on Poetry Day 2025.

Shaffer lives on the island of O'ahu.

Coyote Arts Titles

Gilbert Alter-Gilbert, editor. *Pipe Dreams: The Drug Experience in Literature*

Greg Boyd. *Brotherton's Travels: Memoirs*

R. Eric Gustafson. *A Path Lit by Stars: Reminiscences*

Jefferson Carter. *Free Hugs: New and Selected Poems*

Joe Martin. *Rumi's Mathnavi: A Theatre Adaptation*

Lawrence Millman.

    Goodbye, Ice: Arctic Poems

    Outsider: My Boyhood with Thoreau (illustrated by Geoff Halverson)

Elias Papadimitrakopoulos. *Toothpaste with Chlorophyll | Maritime Hot Baths* (translated from the Greek by John Taylor; illustrated by Alekos Fassianos)

Eric Paul Shaffer.

    Free Speech: poem sequences

    Green Leaves: Selected & New Poems

    A Million-Dollar Bill: Poems

    Second Nature: Poems

Christopher Spranger.

    The Book of Tasks, Volume I: Atlantean Undertakings

    The Comedy of Agony: A Book of Poisonous Contemplations

Leslie Stahlhut. *The Secret of the Old Cloche: Agatha Christine Mystery Stories, #1*

John Taylor. *What Comes from the Night: Poems*

Forthcoming Coyote Arts Titles

Eric Basso. *Fictions: The Beak Doctor: Short Fictions, 1972–1976 &*
   Bartholomew Fair (with an introduction by Jeff VanderMeer)
René Daumal. *The Anti-Heaven* (translated and with an introduction by
   Jordan Jones)
Jordan Jones. *The Wheel: Poems*
Kendall Lappin. *Dead French Poets Speak Plain English & Memoirs of a*
   Translator of Poetry
Joe Martin. *Parabola: Shorter Fictions*
Gérard de Nerval. *Aurélia, followed by Sylvie* (translated by Kendall Lappin
   and with an introduction by Eric Basso)
Eric Paul Shaffer. *GroundWork: The Fires Outside & RattleSnake Rider*
Leslie Stahlhut.
   Borderlands of the Heart and Other Stories
   The Hidden Staircase: Agatha Christine Mystery Stories, #2

www.ingramcontent.com/pod-product-compliance
Lightning Source LLC
Chambersburg PA
CBHW031311060726
47590CB00003B/1161